Hotels

INTERNATIONAL DESIGN PORTFOLIOS

First published in the United States of America by:

Rockport Publishers, Inc.
33 Commercial Street
Gloucester, Massachusetts 01930-5089
Telephone: (978) 282-9590
Facsimile: (978) 283-2742

Distributed to the book trade and art trade in the United States by:

North Light Books, an imprint of
F & W Publications
1507 Dana Avenue
Cincinnati, Ohio 45207
Telephone: (800) 289-0963

Other Distribution by:

Rockport Publishers, Inc.
Gloucester, Massachusetts 01930-5089

ISBN 1-56496-412-4

10 9 8 7 6 5 4 3 2 1

Designer: Jennie R. Bush, Books By Design, Inc.
Front cover image: *Wilson & Associates, The Palace of the Lost City
Bophuthatswana, South Africa*
Back cover images: *(clockwise from top) see pages 23, 61, and 25*

Manufactured in China.

Hotels

INTERNATIONAL DESIGN PORTFOLIOS

ARCHITECTURE EDITOR
ELENA MARCHESO MORENO

ROCKPORT PUBLISHERS
GLOUCESTER, MASSACHUSETTS

Table of Contents

Introduction

On the following pages, a wide variety of new and renovated hotels demonstrate the latest thinking about a unique building type with its own set of characteristics that often consist of psychological as well as practical components. These buildings have one common denominator; all have been designed by architects who bring special talents to a field where their profession's creativity has been sorely needed.

There could be no better time to look at hotels. Construction volume, after a half decade hiatus, is up. A nearly twenty percent annual growth rate makes hotels among the fastest growing building types in the United States. And the recent years have been a time of fundamental change as both designers and managers re-evaluate the ingredients of successful operation.

One significant change is that hotels are built to cater to more-focused markets. During the high-flying 1980s, developers fell over each other in a competition to build luxury-suite facilities until the market was flooded with too much of the same thing. There were many empty rooms when the decade ended. Now developers generally stick to one of four audiences. The most prevalent one is economy travelers. While the facilities built to house them offer more amenities than they might have before the '80s boom, the downside is cookie-cutter standardization and look-alike appearance no matter where they are built. These projects are often carried out by the in-house planners of hotel chains; planners given little leeway for the individuality of character that would interest readers searching for the leading edge of hostelry design shown here.

Three types of hotels in the current generation, however, offer great interest. One thriving type is luxury hotels for business people—especially abroad, although even there they are often run by U.S. chains. Developers tend to employ well-known architects to provide conspicuous allure. The clientele expects to be lavished with high technology rather than old-world elegance. It demands access to electronic communications at every turn, elaborate meeting rooms complete with the latest in virtual reality equipment, and fast rather than elegant service.

The luxury hotel, as developed in the late-nineteenth century, was the grand hotel patronized by people of independent means who arrived with their large families and many servants for long stays. People on business usually went to rooming houses that, at best, supplied clean beds and basic meals. Today, of course, that situation has been turned somewhat on its head. While the globalization of business and forgiving tax laws on related expenses have catapulted a new breed of exacting patron into the high-priced rooms, it is often independent travelers and families who must seek out modest inns and budget-chain facilities.

Resorts form a hostelry category of foremost interest. They currently account for some 40 percent of all bookings and come in a wide variety of types catering to every economic strata. At the high end, not surprisingly, are once again hotels catering to business people. Whether members of the increasingly affluent upper reaches checking in on their own, or a broader group checking in for focus sessions or conventions, these people too want every electronic convenience, presumably to keep on top of the activities they are trying to escape. In resorts of every class, conference centers now take the place of lounges and activity rooms.

But what is really new about resorts of every economic complexion is the way that "escape" is packaged and merchandised. Owners and operators no longer rely on a clientele content to sit on a beach or pursue a single sport, such as golf or skiing. To counter the seasonal nature of these activities and maintain year-round bookings, management now promises "a total escape" to excitement, adventure, and/or romance. The architect may even be asked to provide a fictional setting for the life of the great game hunter or a Spanish conquistador, stretching fantasy to unaccustomed limits.

The final category of activity in hospitality design is the one that promises to revitalize existing resources and, in the process, preserve many landmarks in town and country. It is updating existing hotels and it has become big business with more than a billion dollars spent every year. While the chain operators are carrying out a number of noteworthy and worthwhile renovations of former grande dames, it may be the small "boutique" renovators that are carrying out the most interesting projects, taking over smaller hotels with unconventional layouts and forgoing the chains' formulas for efficient operations. They are producing intimate and distinctive hotels with often moderate room rates.

The architects and interior designers whose work appears in this book bring special gifts that go beyond creativity. They have long experience in matching users' expectations from a building to those of the owners. Guests are attracted to hotels by their exhilarating design—especially when it conveys a heightened sense of their particular locale. In programming these buildings, designers bring functional considerations back to basics when clients stray too far away. For instance, owners understood the need for exhilarating design ever since architect-developer John Portman opened the Atlanta Hyatt Regency in 1965. It's dizzying lobby, soaring to a distant skylit roof and pierced by space rocket elevators brought people from all over the world to gape. Hotels had once again become places to stay instead of the minimal shelter from which travelers quickly moved on as advocated by the efficiency experts who took over design after World War II. Only recently have many owners and operators embraced the idea that hotels should also give guests a firm impression of where they are on the map by incorporating regional characteristics into design—an idea espoused by leading architects since the beginnings of the profession.

But one of the biggest changes since the post-war period has been in the basic design of hotel function. The inviting social spaces and public corridors on the following pages are far removed from the confusing dark routes and spaces guests confronted in the past, when efficiency diagrams without regard to amenity governed planning.

While caring for the guest's good spirits—not to mention their comfort, health, welfare, and safety, and the owners concerns for economy and smooth operations—the designers featured here do what they do best. They produce thoroughly satisfying results.

Charles K. Hoyt, FAIA

Cesar Pelli & Associates Architects, Inc.

1056 CHAPEL STREET
NEW HAVEN, CONNECTICUT 06510

SEA HAWK HOTEL & RESORT FUKUOKA CITY, JAPAN

Cesar Pelli has identified and increased the social value of the buildings he designs. He has demonstrated his concern for the social aspect of aesthetic issues such as the significance of buildings as makers of city silhouettes, and the importance of designs that support an existing city fabric. His widely acclaimed contributions to the practice of architecture are characterized by his belief that buildings should be responsible citizens. His writings and lectures on these subjects are supported by the tangible proof of his designs.

Pelli has avoided formalistic preconceptions in his designs. He believes that the aesthetic qualities of a building should grow from the specific characteristics of each project, such as its location, construction technology, and purpose. In search of the most appropriate response to each project, his designs cover a wide range of solutions and materials.

Cesar Pelli's public spaces have made extraordinary contributions to twentieth-century urban life. His public spaces are conceived as the contemporary counterpart of the Italian piazza in the sixteenth century. This invention answers a critical need and lends increasing value to our cities.

In 1995, the American Institute of Architects awarded Cesar Pelli the Gold Medal, recognizing a lifetime of distinguished achievement and outstanding contributions.

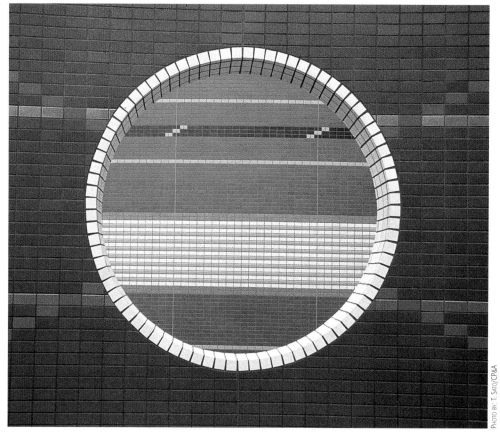

PHOTO BY: T. SATO/CP&A

The design for the Sea Hawk Hotel & Resort in Fukuoka City, Japan, creates a composition of cultural forms. Its lines relate to the water's edge, and its tower becomes a beacon from the sea. Fractured curvilinear forms complement profiles of an adjacent monumental baseball stadium with its three-part retractable roof.

CESAR PELLI & ASSOCIATES ARCHITECTS, INC.

The taut curves of the roof and walls relate to wind and water. The low, earth-bound forms of the dome offer visual balance.

CESAR PELLI & ASSOCIATES ARCHITECTS, INC.

In keeping with a Japanese tradition of economical and durable tile construction, the walls were developed as richly textured and colored tile surfaces. A luminous atrium is filled with fountains and trees, along with a sculptural "tree house": an elevated platform that offers expansive vistas.

13

Arquitectonica

550 BRICKELL AVENUE, SUITE 200
MIAMI, FLORIDA 33131

PLANET HOLLYWOOD ITT HOTEL LAS VEGAS, NEVADA

Arquitectonica is based in Miami, with offices in New York, San Francisco, Paris, Hong Kong, and Shanghai. Since its founding in 1977, Arquitectonica has developed an international practice recognized for excellence and innovation. The firm is best known for its creative ability to design memorable projects with regional identity.

The firm is committed to providing clients cost-saving designs that result in profitable projects for developers and efficiently operated buildings for users. Arquitectonica's principals are directly involved in the design of all projects. These principals and their professional staff of over eighty have won numerous design awards, and their work has been widely published in the business and architectural press.

Their overseas work includes projects on several continents, from complex mixed-use developments, resorts, hotels, retail centers, and office buildings, to specialized projects such as a U.S. Embassy, an opera house, and several bank headquarters.

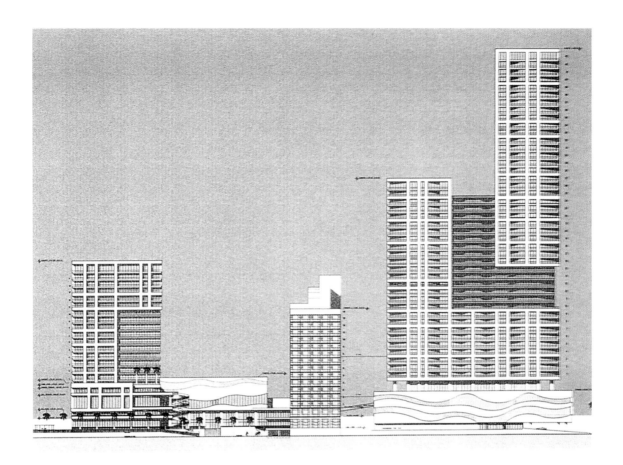

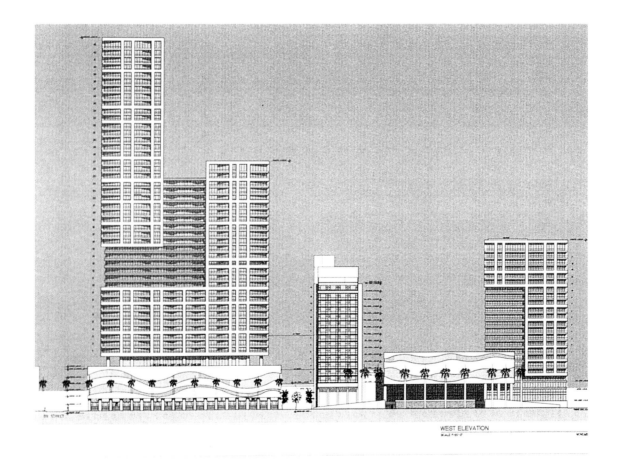

WEST ELEVATION

EWALK HOTEL/RETAIL COMPLEX NEW YORK, NEW YORK

Arrowstreet Inc.

212 ELM STREET
SOMERVILLE, MASSACHUSETTS 02144

Arrowstreet's portfolio includes a broad range of hospitality projects from city-center hotels and conference centers to seaside inns and resort plans. The firm has been successfully completing hospitality projects for over thirty years.

Their site and building design expertise helps to minimize construction costs and maximize the long-term competitive advantage of the resulting facilities. The firm's projects present clear identities, attractive environments, and efficient organizations. Services range from preliminary evaluations of project feasibility and exising facilities to full plans and architectural documents.

Arrowstreet's experience in hospitality design gives them insight into specialized operational and technical issues. They understand the paramount need to serve the customer in an appealing and efficient manner. Equal emphasis is placed in the design of attractive patron spaces and on efficient back-of-the-house areas. Adept at both renovation and new construction, the firm excels at projects posing unique regulatory or technical challenges. Work includes new construction and renovation of hotels, extended-stay lodging, dormitory-type housing, and conference facilities.

HARVARD SQUARE HOTEL CAMBRIDGE, MASSACHUSETTS

Arrowstreet's renovation of the Harvard Square Hotel included new building systems and re-creation of the public spaces and guest rooms, along with a new entrance that faces onto Harvard Square. From the street level entrance, one enters a new two-level space, revealing the upper lobby and the lower cafe.

THE EXCHANGE CONFERENCE CENTER BOSTON, MASSACHUSETTS

This hotel conference center was created from a dilapidated historic building protected by the Boston Landmarks Commission. The gutted shell now houses 20,000 square feet of presentation and meeting space.

ARROWSTREET INC.

21

Barry Design Associates, Inc.

10780 SANTA MONICA BOULEVARD, SUITE 300
LOS ANGELES, CALIFORNIA 90025

HOTEL NIKKO TOKYO TOKYO, JAPAN

Barry Design Associates (BDA) creates outstanding hotels around the world. Never limited by a single design style, nor led by the transience of fleeting trends, BDA designs range from traditional to eclectic to contemporary. No matter the style, BDA designers are known for their ability to transform dreams into unique environments, providing timeless elegance and comfort for hoteliers and their guests.

Award-winning Barry Design Associates specializes in interior and graphic design programs for fine hotels, resorts, restaurants, and deluxe residences worldwide. Their repeat business with some of the world's most respected hotels is testimony to their success.

Working closely with clients, BDA's team of dedicated professionals pays strict attention not only to aesthetics, but also to the budget, schedule, functional space, and market requirements; and performs extensive research on the history of a project's location and people. By incorporating these factors into the overall design concept and intent, Barry Design Associates creates hotels with a unique sense of identity and grace.

The sophisticated elegance of Hotel Nikko Tokyo is immediately apparent upon entering the lobby, above. Pale woods and matte-finished limestone provide luxurious light finishes, and counter the potential for high levels of glare reflected from the adjacent sea.

Two of the hotel's 11 restaurants and lounges are shown here. The Bayside Café, top, evokes images of the ocean, from a tile mosaic of underwater animal life, to lamp fixtures that conjure up undulating seaweed and other plants. The Toh-Gu Restaurant is a modern twist on the traditional design of a Chinese temple.

A calm and elegant seating area off the main lobby continues the theme of light colors.

BARRY DESIGN ASSOCIATES, INC.

The living room of the Presidential Suite
focuses on the vistas of the surrounding
bay. Soft earth-tones, minimal patterns,
and luxe fabrics offer a sense of openness
and calm that is decidedly Oriental.

BARRY DESIGN ASSOCIATES, INC.

Challenged to maintain references to the original design of the architectural visionary Frank Lloyd Wright, the designers established a radial floor patterning when renovating the atrium, left, that is interwoven with sub-patterns reflecting the original surrounding windows. Both the Shuttle Elevator Lobby, bottom left, and the Rainbow Lounge, below, have energetic, contemporary designs, intended to appeal to a young clientele.

BARRY DESIGN ASSOCIATES, INC.

The Imperial Suite is the sometimes home
of the Crown Prince of Japan. From its
granite, anigre, and marble bathroom, to
its rich-colored living-room furnishings,
to the "men's club" look of the wood-
paneled library, this suite, like the hotel,
is world class.

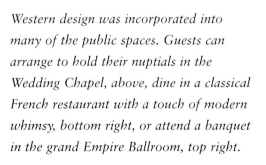

Western design was incorporated into many of the public spaces. Guests can arrange to hold their nuptials in the Wedding Chapel, above, dine in a classical French restaurant with a touch of modern whimsy, bottom right, or attend a banquet in the grand Empire Ballroom, top right.

BARRY DESIGN ASSOCIATES, INC.

Walt Disney Imagineering

1401 FLOWER STREET
GLENDALE, CALIFORNIA 91221-5020

DISNEY'S BOARDWALK INN AND VILLAS ORLANDO, FLORIDA

Walt Disney Imagineering makes it their business to give form to dreams. From the moment a new hotel development project begins, Disney's designers plan spaces intended to invite the hotel patrons inside, then embrace them each in the true fashion and comfort afforded the most welcome guests.

While officially the developers, and thus the clients of subsequent design firms, Walt Disney Imagineering staff lead the design theme of each hotel project. From site plan to floor plan to exterior elevation concepts to interior decoration, the Disney design staff sets the project in motion. Then they hand their creative concepts over to consultants for further development.

PHOTOS BY PETER AARON/ESTO

CREDITS

DEVELOPER: *Walt Disney Imagineering, Lake Buena Vista, FL*
DESIGN ARCHITECT: *Robert A.M. Stern, New York, NY*
ARCHITECT OF RECORD: *HKS Architects, Dallas, TX*

INTERIOR DESIGN: *Sue Firestone & Associates, Santa Barbara, CA*
ART DESIGN & ARTIFACTS: *Parker Blake, Inc., Castle Rock, CO*
LIGHTING DESIGN: *Lighting Design Alliance, Los Angeles, CA*

The dramatic entry tower, left, is Walt Disney Imagineering's signature stroke in the main entry lobby, and sets the tone for the charm and warmth found throughout the interiors. A reminder that elegance can be casual, inviting, and fun, flower-headed people-chairs are sure to keep the hearth a main focus in the lobby, right.

The references to a New England seaside resort are unmistakable on the vibrant face the BoardWalk Inn turns to the waterfront.

Robert A.M. Stern Architects

460 WEST 34TH STREET
NEW YORK, NEW YORK 10010

Robert A.M. Stern is a 108-person firm of architects, landscape architects, interior designers, and supporting staff. Over its twenty-seven year history, Robert A.M. Stern Architects has established an international reputation as a leading design firm with wide experience in residential, commercial, and institutional work. As the firm's practice has diversified, its geographic scope has widened to include current projects in Europe and Asia, in addition to the United States.

Robert A.M. Stern Architects has earned global recognition through numerous awards and citations for design excellence. The firm has received the National Honor Award of the American Institute of Architects four times. Stern and his staff design close to $200,000,000 of construction each year. They currently have projects underway in 12 states and Japan.

THE BOARDWALK INN ORLANDO, FLORIDA

Photo by Peter Aaron/ESTO

Varied in the manner that the architecture of any small town might be, the BoardWalk completes a Disney lakeside resort district. The hotel's design takes a bow to the rambling hotels often found in New England at the turn of the century.

ROBERT A.M. STERN ARCHITECTS

*Garden courts and a series of intercon-
nected small-scale buildings, above,
reinforce the concept of a small, seaside
vacation town. A meeting facility, right,
takes its cue from Gothic-inspired
Victorian architecture, adding to the
BoardWalk town's architectural collage.*

Facing towards the canal, the buildings take on a larger scale, with wide roof overhangs and bold horizontals. A central pool serves as a gathering spot, below.

ROBERT A.M. STERN ARCHITECTS

Sue Firestone & Associates

4141 STATE STREET, SUITE B-13
SANTA BARBARA, CALIFORNIA 93110

THE **BOARDWALK INN** ORLANDO, FLORIDA

PHOTO BY ROBERT MILLER

The interior design firm of Sue Firestone & Associates specializes in custom-design services for luxury residences, resorts, and selected hotels. Throughout her twenty-two years in the industry, Sue Firestone has gained international recognition for her designs. For 20 years, she led the hospitality design organization Design 1 Interiors.

Sue Firestone and her design staff work to ensure the fulfillment of each client's project goals and visions. Their interiors combine timeless design and detail. These professionals believe that there are no substitutes for integrity and high quality in every task they undertake. They understand the demands of their clients' busy schedules and help to ease the frustration and time requirements that are often associated with the design and development of a project.

The collection of art and artifacts scattered throughout the main lobby and guest reception, conference center pre-function area, and members attic lounge are rooted in the American vacation experience of the early 20th-century.

PHOTO BY ROBERT MILLER

The Presidential Suite, left, below, and top right, is elegant with its curving architectural features, and "collectible" artifacts. A typical guest room and bath, below right.

SUE FIRESTONE & ASSOCIATES

SUE FIRESTONE & ASSOCIATES

Birch Coffey Design Associates, Inc.

206 EAST 63RD STREET, SUITE 3
NEW YORK, NEW YORK 10021

THE CENTURY

Birch Coffey Design Associates is a full-service interior design firm dedicated to producing creative design solutions for the hospitality, restaurant, and club industries. Since its establishment in 1987, the firm has achieved an outstanding reputation for design excellence and client service. The broad range of domestic and international projects conducted by the firm reflects the diversified interests and professional experience of its founder, Birch Coffey. During his twenty years of practice, he has been responsible for an impressive roster of design-driven commissions that include luxury hotels and cruise ships, residential building lobbies and country clubs, and prestigious offices.

The firm's success can be largely attributed to its ability to recognize market trends and directions, and to interpret those concepts into spaces that are distinctive and that promote the overall product. Birch Coffey's design solutions strike a balance among the primary concerns facing all hospitality endeavors. The potential for each property—new or existing—is evaluated to create its best "total image." Attention to detail and a deep sense of commitment are qualities shared by the firm's ten architects and design professionals.

The circular layout and flow of the café eating areas assure comfortable and efficient passenger service on the Century, one of Celebrity Cruises' newest luxury liners.

39

BIRCH COFFEY DESIGN ASSOCIATES, INC.

Dining and public areas were designed to appeal to a broad customer base, one that includes younger cruisers.

BIRCH COFFEY DESIGN ASSOCIATES, INC.

A contemporary interpretation of traditional "cruise style," complete with interactive technology, was designed to appeal to vacationers in the upper end of the mass market.

BIRCH COFFEY DESIGN ASSOCIATES, INC.

BIRCH COFFEY DESIGN ASSOCIATES, INC.

Gracious living was the design theme for the living suites. A warm color palette and warm woods are part of the luxurious accommodations of the Century.

Brennan Beer Gorman/Architects
Brennan Beer Gorman Monk/Interiors

515 MADISON AVENUE
NEW YORK, NEW YORK 10022

Winning international accolades for their hotel renovations, Brennan Beer Gorman/Architects and Brennan Beer Gorman Monk/Interiors have recently completed projects that include more than 10,000 guest rooms and related facilities in some of the world's most recognized hotels.

Whether reflagging the property or renovating to keep pace with the marketplace, Brennan Beer Gorman/Architects and Brennan Beer Gorman Monk/Interiors adhere to the principal that hotel renovation means creating a strategic master plan that addresses the challenges of the changing financial, operational, and aesthetic standards in the modern hospitality market. They remain sensitive to the realities of budget, schedule, and existing physical conditions, and committed to improving the guest experience and the hotel's operating efficiency.

The firm's hotel renovation portfolio includes The St. Regis, The Carlton, Essex House, Hotel Nikko New York, Sherry-Netherland, and numerous other landmark hotels.

CROWNE PLAZA WASHINGTON, D.C.

44

The fifteen-million-dollar renovation of this historic Beaux Arts building in Washington, D.C., includes a new scalloped-glass canopy, far left, that harmonizes with the decorative exterior elements, yet still respects the integrity of the original facade. The barrel-vaulted ceiling inside the lobby closely resembles its original splendor.

The hotel's expansion to 318 guest rooms was made possible by a new, two-story addition, accommodating forty Club-level rooms and a lounge. The architects employed a light-weight steel system for the expansion so that the structure of the vintage building would not be overpowered.

45

One of Southeast Asia's most grand hotels, The Peninsula, provides the nostalgic ambiance of a haven for weary travelers. With this spirit in mind, the designers renovated the restaurants and bar with stone and wood floors, ceiling fans, and light fabrics and finishes for subtle drama and unmistakable comfort.

ALL PHOTOS BY ANTHONY ALBARELLO

BRENNAN BEER GORMAN

PHOTO BY DAVID AUBRY

Washington, D.C.'s prominent Ritz-Carlton Hotel was restored to its grand, though somewhat eclectic, early 1900s style. The lobby, left, is separated into two intimately scaled levels.

PHOTO BY DAVID AUBRY

47

BRENNAN BEER GORMAN

Aiello Associates, Inc.

1525 MARKET STREET, SUITE A
DENVER, COLORADO 80202

For over thirty years, Aiello Associates has been addressing the challenges of architectural interior design. Accolades attest to the firm's dedication to personal service, attention to detail, and understanding of each client's individual needs. The firm's superior design talent makes the difference in the ultimate success of each project.

Times have changed and markets have become even more critical to target. Aiello Associates' design teams know how to create effective designs that take into consideration image, efficiency, and the bottom line of their clients. The firm's scope of work spans from high-end full-service luxury resorts to restaurants, casinos, entertainment facilities, ski resorts, and commercial buildings.

The spirit of teamwork maximizes the exceptional contribution of each member of the firm. Timeless designs, creativity, functionality, and value are goals the Aiello design team strives for in each project. High professional standards that ensure the creation of trust-based relationships is one of the many reasons why Aiello Associates has maintained the respect of its clients and the design community for decades.

PHOTO BY: PHILLIP NILSSON

Both the Poco Diablo Resort in Arizona, above, and Furnace Creek Inn Resort in California, right, make use of regional materials and local design aesthetics to create comfortable environments.

In its downtown Denver setting, the Westin Hotel Tabor Center was designed to function especially for the business traveler.

FURNACE CREEK INN RESORT DEATH VALLEY, CALIFORNIA

PHOTO BY: CHAD SLATTERY

49

AIELLO ASSOCIATES, INC.

Cheryl Rowley Interior Design

9538 BRIGHTON WAY, SUITE 316
BEVERLY HILLS, CALIFORNIA 90210

HOTEL MONACO SAN FRANCISCO, CALIFORNIA

A fourteen-member specialty firm, Cheryl Rowley Interior Design directs its attention to luxury hotels, distinctive restaurants, and fine private homes.

The firm's work in California has been much celebrated, but Cheryl Rowley Interior Design's reach extends far beyond the coast. Many of Rowley's projects have received multiple awards. This stems in large part, according to Cheryl Rowley, less from making statements than from realizing what is appropriate in each individual case; appropriate to the owner, management, and budget, as well as to the marketplace.

Cheryl Rowley's stock in trade is her design sense—an exciting, eclectic approach born in California and broadened during extensive travel through Europe, the Pacific, and the Far East. Her work is characterized by a light, sophisticated ambiance, natural materials, high style, and a relaxed feeling of welcome, comfort, and grace.

PHOTOS COURTESY OF CHERYL ROWLEY INTERIOR DESIGN

Classical Greek architecture, rich, saturated Mediterranean colors, and exotic furniture all inspire thoughts of journeys afar at the Hotel Monaco, San Francisco.

50

*Free-spirited public spaces and fantastical
guest rooms give form to Rowley's vision
of the Hotel Monaco as an exploring ship,
having plied the farthest oceans of the
world for treasures, now at rest and
swelled with its booty.*

CHERYL ROWLEY INTERIOR DESIGN

53

CHERYL ROWLEY INTERIOR DESIGN

The chic new incarnation of the Beverly Prescott Hotel, Los Angeles, is an elegant urban oasis in a Beverly Hills residential neighborhood.

CHERYL ROWLEY INTERIOR DESIGN

Some living room views at the Beverly Prescott Hotel.

CHERYL ROWLEY INTERIOR DESIGN

Rich colors of coral, rose, and cream com-
bine with mahogany and cherry woods in
the hotel's 10 suites.

57

Einhorn Yaffee Prescott Architecture and Engineering

THE ARGUS BUILDING
BROADWAY AT BEAVER STREET
ALBANY, NEW YORK 12201

THE EQUINOX MANCHESTER, VERMONT

Restore. Preserve. Reconstruct. Rehabilitate. Adapt. These are ways to give new life to older buildings. Einhorn Yaffee Prescott is an architecture, engineering, and interior design firm that leads in the preservation and restoration of older buildings. They have worked extensively on historic preservation and adaptive re-use projects, documenting and renewing landmarks and monuments and adapting other architecturally important buildings to serve new uses. Their approach is to balance preservation requirements with the demand for modern educational, corporate, medical, and civic space. With a pragmatic approach, technical skills, and sensitive integration of modern systems, they help to preserve the designs of our architectural forebears and to assure their continued future.

The firm is nationally noted for its continued contribution to the preservation of the nation's historic landmarks. Among them are the Lincoln and Jefferson Memorials, the Amphitheater at Arlington Cemetery, Federal Hall, the Washington Monument, and the Old Executive Office Building.

Once the summer home of Mrs. Abraham Lincoln and then guest hotel to four U.S. Presidents, the Equinox is a cherished Vermont landmark. Twenty-million dollars was spent to preserve the historic fabric of the building and expand its guest rooms and public facilities. A new addition is shown at right. Above is an image of the original hotel.

EINHORN YAFFEE PRESCOTT ARCHITECTURE AND ENGINEERING

Carefully executed restoration in the public spaces re-creates the hotel's original ambiance.

EINHORN YAFFEE PRESCOTT ARCHITECTURE AND ENGINEERING

New spaces such as the dining area, above. Like the moldings, mantels, paneling, arches, and ceilings, the wooden stairways were meticulously restored, left.

Design Continuum, Inc.

5 PIEDMONT CENTER, SUITE 300
ATLANTA, GEORGIA 30305

Design Continuum is an Atlanta-based firm specializing in the design of hotels, restaurants, private city clubs and country clubs. Their twenty-five years of hospitality design experience and careful attention to detail enables them to provide successful interiors for urban hotels, convention and conference properties, and major destination resorts throughout the United States, Canada, Europe, and Japan.

In addition to creativity and enthusiasm, Design Continuum's commitment to providing excellent personal service has resulted in a prominent reputation and a continuing list of repeat clients. Their knowledge of the process of hotel and club design results in close coordination with the architect, lighting designer, general contractor, and other consultants. The firm's varied experience offers competence in a variety of design styles including historic restorations, adaptive reuse, transitional, eclectic, and contemporary idioms.

PHOTO BY MILROY & MCALEER

The elegance of the lobby of the Hotel Inter-Continental Los Angeles is softly modern and very inviting, with contemporary artworks on permanent display.

DESIGN CONTINUUM, INC.

The creatively lighted ceiling coffers of the Grand Ballroom nicely satisfy the requirements of both meeting and banquet functions, far right. Mixed genres in the public spaces and the California-style suites, below, all add up to the West Coast comfort.

DESIGN CONTINUUM, INC.

ALL PHOTOS BY: MILROY & MCALLEER

65

The sophisticated club ambiance of the 211-room Hotel Inter-Continental Toronto is derived from warm wood tones, sparkling brass and crystal, cool marble floors, walls and accents, and colors of rose and moss green. This rich warmth washes the hotel interiors from the lobby to the guest rooms.

ALL PHOTOS BY ROBERT MILLER

67

Cooper Carry, Inc.

3520 PIEDMONT ROAD NE, SUITE 200
ATLANTA, GA 30305-1595

Cooper Carry has established a reputation for thoughtful design that encompasses a wide range of project types, including hotels, offices, retail centers, housing academic buildings, medical facilities, town centers, and master plans. Since its founding in 1960, Cooper Carry has developed into a firm of three design professional services: architecture, interior architecture/facility programming, and landscape architecture/planning. This internal structure helps them integrate the design of a building to its site and intended function, resulting in high-quality, holistic design services that many of the nation's most prestigious corporations, developers, universities, and public agencies enjoy. The firm's client list includes IBM, AT&T, Bell South, Barnett Banks, Kimberly Clark, Siemens, Prentiss, and Prudential.

In the last twenty-five years, Cooper Carry has received over 50 design awards, including 18 from the American Institute of Architects. In 1987, the firm received the AIA Silver Medal of the Georgia Association AIA, which is awarded for 10 years of consistent design excellence. While Cooper Carry's projects vary in size, scope, complexity, location, and design solution, the firm's commitment to design excellence is a common denominator that unifies its work.

BRASSTOWN VALLEY RESORT YOUNG HARRIS, GEORGIA

There is little doubt that Cooper Carry architects successfully met their design goals of creating a project that incorporates local craftsmanship and appears as if it had always been a part of its site. The Brasstown Valley Resort for the Georgia Department of Parks and Natural Resources was designed for maximum comfort with a mountain-life theme.

69

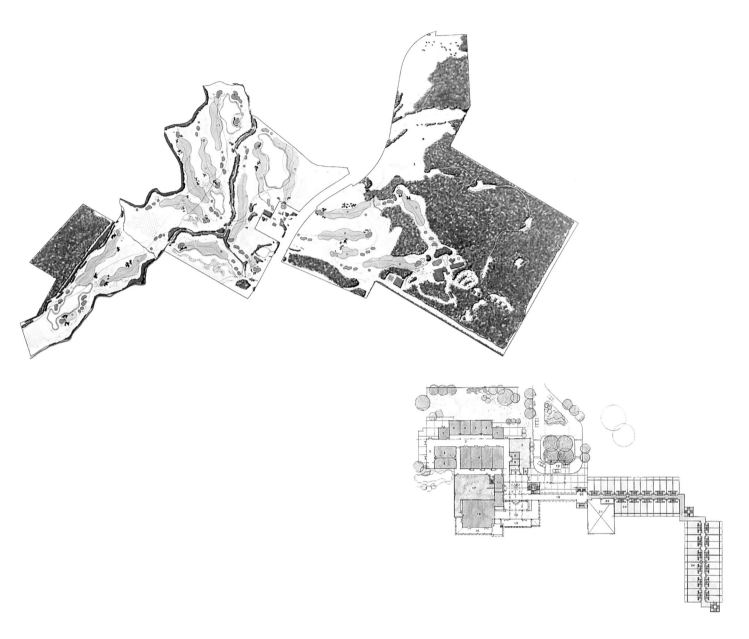

A 106-room lodge and eight four-bedroom cottages are surrounded by woodland flowers, native trees, and stone outcroppings.

COOPER CARRY, INC.

Guests can enjoy the woods from their private balconies, or gather together in the lobby and lounge, above. In addition to an indoor pool, right, another is found outside. Other recreational amenities include a golf course and club house, playground, and health club.

71

The Norwalk Waterside Convention Center and Marriot consists of two components—a twenty-three-story hotel and conference center. It was conceived as the focal point for the developing downtown waterfront.

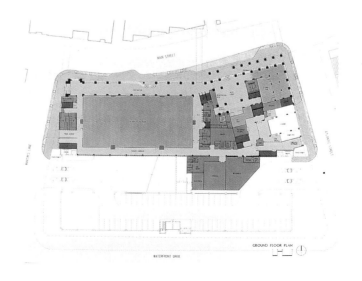

The 110,000 sq. ft. conference facility has a 15,000 sq. ft. exhibit hall, two ball-rooms, and additional meeting spaces,left. Transparency at the entry helps advertise the buildings exhibits. The lobby, below.

73

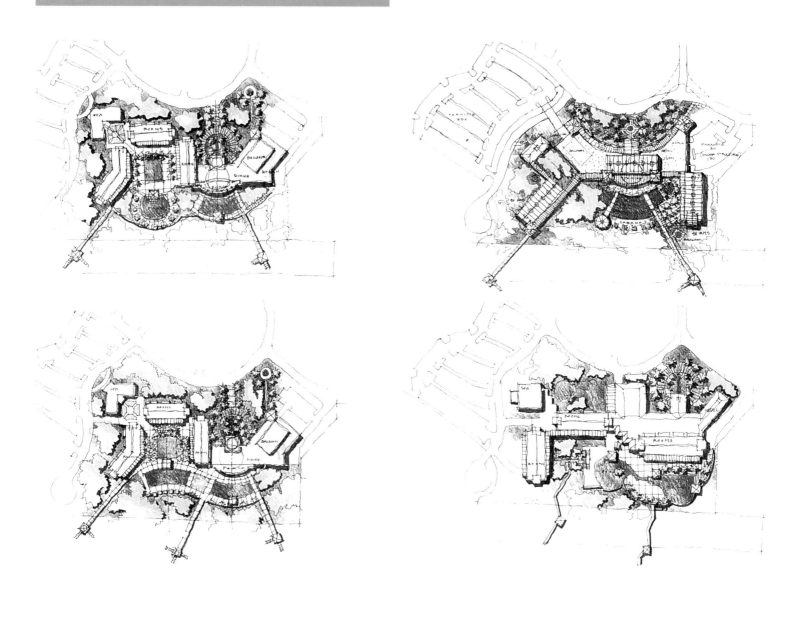

Designs for the Kiawah Island Resort at Kiawah Island, South Carolina, are centered on the concept of a village clustered along the coastline.

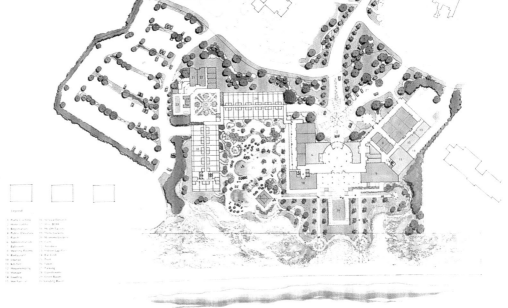

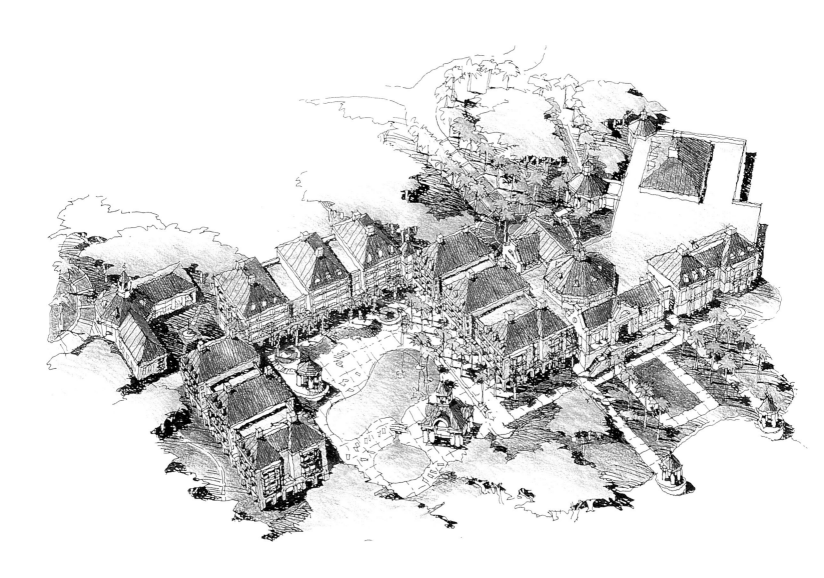

75

Hamilton Hochheiser Ross

6011 STAPLES MILL ROAD
RICHMOND, VIRGINIA 23228

FORT MAGRUDER INN WILLIAMSBURG, VIRGINIA

With over 20 years of combined talents in architectural interiors for the hospitality industry, Hamilton Hochheiser Ross has a solid reputation for high-quality design.

The firm's two principals, Tom Hamilton and Carole Hochheiser Ross, each oversee their staff of architects and interior designers. Both principals are actively involved with every project, working closely with their in-house teams.

At the core of the firm's philosophy is an intense appreciation for the architecture of a space. Whether the project entails new construction or refurbishment, Hamilton Hochheiser Ross delivers solutions with a great deal of visual impact. A close knowledge of the hospitality industry ensures this design success.

Award-winning designs have led to the firm's recognition and listing in *Who's Who in Hotel Design.* Hamilton Hochheiser Ross is among the top twenty-five percent of hospitality giants listed by *Interior Design.*

Two views of the lobby, above and top right, of the Fort Magruder Inn, Williamsburg, Virginia, highlight a blend of Colonial colors in a contemporary space.

76

DOUBLETREE HOTEL METAIRE, LOUISIANA

The design of the DoubleTree Hotel in Metaire, near New Orleans, offers a blend of New Orleans and classical design styles.

Di Leonardo International, Inc.

2350 POST ROAD
WARWICK, RHODE ISLAND 02886

Di Leonardo International, Inc. has established itself as one of the most prominent hospitality interior design firms in the world. Its reputation stems from the quality of its work and a consistently outstanding level of service for hotels/resorts, casinos, restaurants, club houses, conference centers, banquet facilities, airports, and cruise ships.

Di Leonardo International ensures smooth transition from a project's conceptual stage through its successful completion by offering schematic design, design development, construction documentation, budget control, and project administration. By carefully controlling and administering each stage of a project, the firm provides its clients problem-free and exceptional service.

Di Leonardo International's full range of interior design capabilities include architectural design, graphic design, lighting design, acoustical design, furnishing specification, menu design, kitchen design, environmental psychology/market research, art/accessory selection, and purchasing.

Guided by the belief that whether new construction or renovation, every end product should be aesthetically pleasing, operationally efficient, and designed to transform investment into profit, the firm's designers have a thorough understanding of the hospitality marketplace. Di Leonardo International's years of international design experience for clients throughout the industry have taught the firm to design profitable facilities exceptionally well.

WESTIN HOTEL PROVIDENCE, RHODE ISLAND

The Westin Hotel in Providence, Rhode Island, serves as a major business convention center for this area of New England. The Rotunda lobby and main lobby stairs are graced with Corinthian-style columns, and the lobby's domed ceiling repeats itself in the health club, all inspired by the impressive architectural history of Rhode Island.

79

A variety of comfortable lounges and restaurants offer business guests a choice of mood during the evening.

DI LEONARDO INTERNATIONAL, INC.

PHOTOS BY WARREN JAGGER

Spacious suites are traditionally furnished.

81

*Contemporary, sophisticated design
prevails at the New World Hotel, in
Makati-Metro, Manila, Philippines.*

DI LEONARDO INTERNATIONAL, INC.

The grand stairway and massive, two-story granite columns in the lobby help set the stage for a five-star hotel experience.

All Photos by Arthur Kan

Waterfalls and collecting pools offer calm respites, as in the coffee shop.

DI LEONARDO INTERNATIONAL, INC.

For the renovation of the New World Hotel in Kowloon, Hong Kong, additional area above the lobby, was secured to create a dramatic two-volume space, left. A modern escalator becomes a design element, connecting the lobby, to a lower meeting level, below.

PHOTO BY JAIME ARDILES, ARCE

PHOTO BY DIMENSIONS MAGAZINE PHOTOGRAPHER

PHOTO BY DIMENSIONS MAGAZINE PHOTOGRAPHER

DI LEONARDO INTERNATIONAL, INC.

Stouffers Concourse Hotel at Hartsfield International Airport, Atlanta, Georgia, with its atrium garden court and private dining areas, is helping to create a new traditional style for Southern hospitality.

DI LEONARDO INTERNATIONAL, INC.

Guestrooms were designed with traditional style and twenty-first-century comfort in mind.

Di Leonardo International, Inc.

Hill/Glazier Architects

700 WELCH ROAD
PALO ALTO, CALIFORNIA 94304

Hill/Glazier Architects specializes in the design of international resorts and hotels. Since 1980, Hill/Glazier has been a prominent, full-service firm providing master planning, environmental and site analyses, schematic design, design development, construction documents, and construction contract administration.

Each design is backed by the experience of more than three hundred projects in fifteen countries and thirty-five states. These projects include unique destination resorts on sensitive ecological sites, high-rise urban hotels, mixed-use resort/residential, and distinctive retail and commercial facilities.

Hill/Glazier has received wide acclaim for its sensitivity to historic traditions, the natural environment, and aesthetic concerns in each project's community. This consideration of the local context and careful planning help the firm create projects with their own sense of place. Hill/Glazier has received numerous national and international awards, and has been featured in a wide variety of publications in the United States and abroad.

The overall composition of the site of the Hualalai Four Seasons Resorts in Kona, Hawaii, with its public buildings and bungalows, evokes the informal Hawaiian villages of the turn-of-the-century.

88

HILL/GLAZIER ARCHITECTS

Hotel and bungalow forms are varied, creating unexpected discovery around every bend at Hualala. All guest rooms have direct access to ocean views, below.

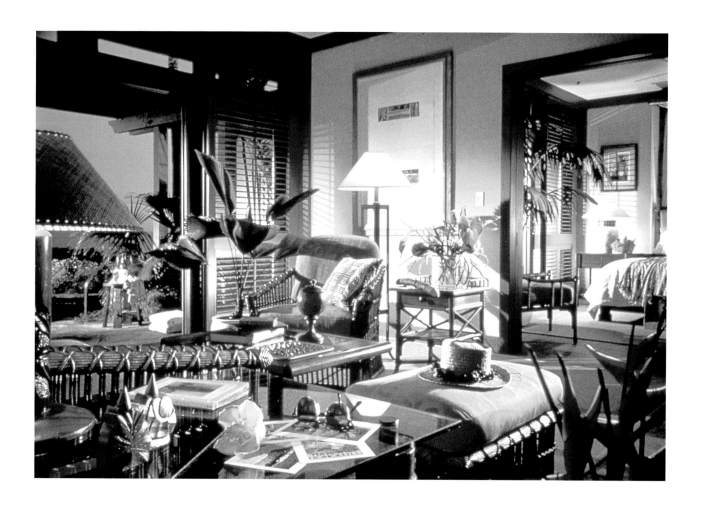

HILL/GLAZIER ARCHITECTS

Located in Santa Monica, Shutters on the Beach recalls the historic resorts and craftsman-style cottages of the Southern California coast at the turn of the century.

The 575-room Hyatt Regency Hill Country Resort in San Antonio, Texas, has traditional limestone facades, wood porches, and other typically Texas Territorial-style features. Two massive stone fireplaces welcome guests to the lobby.

SCRIPPS LA JOLLA HOTEL LA JOLLA, CALIFORNIA

Scripps La Jolla Hotel, California, will combine three dissimilar old structures with new buildings in a consistent and unified design scheme.

HALF MOON BAY RESORT CALIFORNIA

This resort at Half Moon Bay, California, is intended to conjure up images of the grand seaside lodges of the late nineteenth century.

93

Knauer Inc.

741 St. Johns Avenue
Highland Park, Illinois 60035

MILWAUKEE HILTON MILWAUKEE, WISCONSIN

Knauer Inc. is a leader in hospitality architecture and design. The company's creativity and years of experience provide a focused, concept-development approach that results in unified design packages that meet the ever-changing needs of the hotel market.

Established in 1984, Knauer has completed hundreds of diversified hospitality projects—new hotels, hotel renovations, casinos, restaurants, convention centers, retail stores, and meeting facilities. Common threads of design excellence and client satisfaction weave throughout their work. They have achieved international recognition through numerous awards, yet their focus remains on the building user. They say their goal is not for a hotel guest to walk into a space and immediately be "wowed," but rather to remember the whole experience of their stay in terms of comfortable space, leaving only with the desire to return.

Designed in 1928 in the Empire style by Holabird and Roche, the Milwaukee Hilton had suffered years of neglect. When Knauer, Inc., stepped in to reclaim the landmark hotel, they improved traffic patterns in the lobby, above, without sacrificing any of the original architectural details. Gold and silver leaf highlight the lobby's Art Deco motif, as do period fabrics, furnishings, and the original marble floors, left. The rich wood-tones of the lobby appear elsewhere, as in the English Room, right.

95

The grand staircase, above, joining the
ballrooms was uncovered and restored
according to Holabird and Roche's original details. The rich colors and elegance of
the original design are revealed in the ball-
rooms, facing page, top, and guest rooms,
right.

KNAUER INC.

This Lake Geneva, Wisconsin, resort was entirely revitalized within twelve months. In a bold move, the lobby was relocated from a tiny inconspicuous space to what was previously the indoor pool, to take full advantage of the magnificent view.

GRAND GENEVA RESORT AND SPA LAKE GENEVA, WISCONSIN

97

New restaurants and a wellness spa were added to the resort, and a number of guest rooms were reconfigured to create suites.

HLW International

115 5TH AVENUE
NEW YORK, NEW YORK 10003

HLW International's focus is to provide creative facilities solutions based on its clients' business goals. With a staff of 240 professionals in New York, the Middle East, Europe, and the Pacific Rim, HLW provides comprehensive services in architecture, engineering, planning, interior architecture, and landscape architecture.

As a full-service organization, HLW offers a collaborative, integrated approach to project design and delivery. The advantages to their clients are clear: faster coordination among specialists with one project management group, more direct communication and innovation grounded in an understanding of team goals, fewer outside consultants, and ultimately a smoother path to project success.

LA PALESTRA NEW YORK, NEW YORK

The once grand old ballroom of the Hotel Des Artistes in Manhattan was transformed by HLW International into La Palestra Center for Preventative Medicine, which is a cross between a physical fitness and medical fitness facility. Many elements of the ballroom's gracious grandeur were restored.

PHOTOS BY: SCOTT FRANCES

Some elements of an old conference room, right, can be found in the new exercise area, top.

New elements at La Palestra were carefully inserted into the shell. These include ribbed-wood ceilings, warm steel walls, and a gallery of mirrors under the skylight. Their purpose is to delineate different scales and different activities, with patient support areas, technical offices, and consultation rooms organized around the main treatment areas.

107

ALL PHOTOS BY: PETER PAIGE

The Equinox is the prototype for a new series of hotel/spa installations in select U.S. cities, including New York. HLW created the first floor reception and lobby area to immediately set the tone for the fitness facility with an elegant, illuminated canopy flanked with torches.

Fitness and spa services, and medical and training support occupy the second and upper floors. A stainless steel stair connects the floors. Next in line after this prototype is the fitness, spa, and retail facility at New York's The Barbizon Hotel.

109

Hughes Design Associates

1487 CHAIN BRIDGE ROAD
McLEAN, VIRGINIA 22101

FOUR SEASONS HOTEL   PHILADELPHIA, PENNSYLVANIA

Hughes Design Associates is a highly respected design firm known throughout North America for specializing in prestigious custom interiors. Since its founding in 1978, the firm has been designing, refurbishing, and restoring hotels, resorts, clubs, restaurants, and other commercial properties.

Steadfast attention to quality and design are consistent throughout all of Hughes Design Associates' projects. Their goal is to execute a successful project—one that is not only on time and within budget, but is also guided smoothly from concept through final installation.

Hughes' services include concept development, space utilization planning and analysis, interior architecture, and furniture and furnishings specification and acquisition. Among the firm's recent projects are the Four Seasons Hotel, Philadelphia; Ritz-Carlton Laguna Niguel, California; ANA Hotel, Washington, D.C.; The Pierre, New York; and Trump Taj Mahal Casino Resort, Atlantic City.

The updated lobby and guest rooms of the Four Seasons Hotel, Philadelphia, are elegantly appointed with rich textiles and furnishings.

110

Two of Washington, D.C.'s more prominent hotels—The Renaissance Mayflower, above, and the Capital Hilton—were recently refurbished by Hughes.

HUGHES DESIGN ASSOCIATES

CAPITOL HILTON WASHINGTON, D.C.

HUGHES DESIGN ASSOCIATES

Part of the ITT Luxury Collection, The Carlton's guest rooms and suites were given classical, elegant updates. Hughes also refurbished the tea lounge, ballroom terrace, and meeting rooms.

Pamela Temples Interiors Inc.

7652 ASHLEY PARK COURT, SUITE 306
ORLANDO, FLORIDA 32835

With decades of collective experience, Pamela Temples Interiors has become one of the most awarded design firms in the hospitality industry. Offering service from comprehensive on-site evaluation to turn-key design services for new construction and renovations, they have produced interior design solutions that warmly welcome travelers to such destinations as the Hyatt Regency Grand Cypress in Orlando; the Marriott Harbor Beach in Ft. Lauderdale; the Calima Resort in Colombia, South America; the Mountain Loft Resort in the Tennessee Smoky Mountains; and Bluebeard's Castle in St. Thomas.

Just five years ago, the firm was only Pamela Temples McMullen and one other designer. Today, they number more than thirty-five. That rapid growth and success is attributed to their goal of affordable design excellence.

Bluebeard's Tower, which dates back to the 1600s, is one of St. Thomas' oldest structures. It was successfully incorporated into a hotel in the 1930s. The transformed lobby appears above.

116

PAMELA TEMPLES INTERIORS INC.

Refreshing colors create a serene atmosphere at the Spa of the Buena Vista Palace.

PAMELA TEMPLES INTERIORS INC.

The Villas of Grand Cypress greet guests
with a warm color palette and cozy
furniture in tranquil surroundings.

PAMELA TEMPLES INTERIORS INC.

Wilson & Associates

3811 TURTLE CREEK BOULEVARD
DALLAS, TEXAS 75219

Wilson & Associates stands out for its diverse experience, its reputation for innovative design, and its understanding that design is a business as well as an art.

Founded in 1975 by current president Trisha Wilson, the firm specializes in commercial projects. Wilson & Associates has designed and installed more than 100,000 guest rooms in 200 hotels worldwide. This design firm integrates the skills of architects and interior designers to offer clients a full scope of services necessary to produce a project, from initial space planning and design through construction documents, furniture purchase, art selection, and move-in.

Wilson & Associates is consistently named among the top three interior design firms in the world by industry professionals, and receives top honors annually in design competitions for both new and historical renovation. Wilson & Associates is a five-time winner of the prestigious American Hotel and Motel Associations Gold Key Award for excellence in hotel design, and for five consecutive years has taken top honors in Lodging Hospitality's Designer Circle Awards Program.

THE PALACE OF THE LOST CITY BOPHUTHATSWANA, SOUTH AFRICA

The temperate climate and the invented concept of a palace in a lost city drove the design theme of this hotel. The Palace of the Lost City is designed around courtyards, open corridors, lofty shaded spaces, and walls that are left totally open to the breeze, above, left, and far left inset. Open air domes atop the hotel's towers are executed in the forms of elephant tusks and palm fronds, far left.

Keeping a close eye on cultural context, the designers continued to focus on creating a palace fit for a king, as is evident in this guest room, above and right.

Pairs of sculpted elephant tusks flank the walls of a lounge, framing small groups of seating, below. References to the African setting are also evident in guest rooms, many of which include the King Suite living room, right.

This international hotel occupies the ground floor plus floors 49 through 70 of the Landmark Tower in Yokohama, Japan's tallest skyscraper. Contemporary artwork juxtaposed against more traditional furnishings and a breathtaking vista result in the serene, but upbeat, Sky Lounge.

Despite the premium of space in Japan, a
voluminously scaled lobby is crafted into
an impressive two-story room. Luxurious
materials are classically and simply
detailed in warm-beige tones throughout
the hotel to allow for sophisticated fabrics
and furnishings and to showcase museum-
quality artwork.

Traditional design, with a French
influence as in the Chapel, left,
unify diverse spaces.

125

A variety of lounges and restaurants offer
hotel guests attractive eating options.

Like the rest of the hotel, guest room floors exhibit elegant architectural details and furnishings.

129

Murphy/Jahn

35 EAST WACKER DRIVE 3RD FLOOR
CHICAGO, ILLINOIS 60601

HOTEL KEMPINSKI MUNICH, GERMANY

Murphy/Jahn has spent 20 years on organization building, and has succeeded in combining design creativity with corporate professionalism. The growing national and international reputation of Murphy/Jahn has led to commissions across the United States, Europe, Africa, and Asia. Their commitment to design excellence and to improvement of the urban environment has been recognized globally for design innovation, vitality, and integrity.

The diversity of Murphy/Jahn's work—high-rise buildings, airport master plans, transportation facilities, urban planning, low-rise commercial projects—stimulates a cross-fertilization of ideas when resolving new architectural challenges. The firm has evolved steadily under the leadership of Helmut Jahn, recognized by the American Institute of Architects as one of the 10 most influential living American architects.

The first building in the Neutral Zone
of Munich Airport, the Hotel Kempinski,
left, serves as a link to the existing
terminal facilities and those that will
follow. Its orthogonal plan is organized
to correspond to the airport level system,
yet it stands alone as a stage set for
entertainment, relaxation, shopping,
and cultural events.

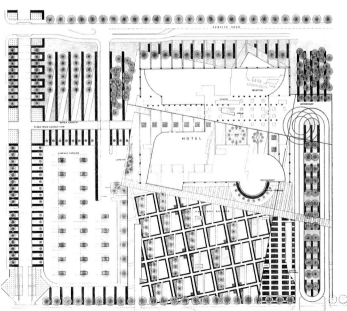

The transparency of cable-supported end walls and free-standing "geranium walls" provides continuity between private hotel spaces in the entrance lobby and the more public reception hall area, the entrance to "the airport city."

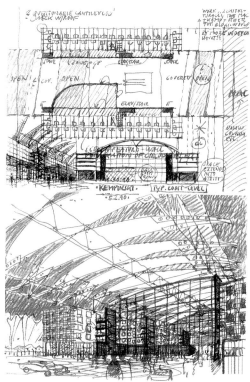

The design centers on integrating the building landscape into the airport. Open, covered, and enclosed "rooms" draw the surrounding landscape into the architecture. A rich sequence of forms, spaces, and colors creates a visual collage that breaks down the expected division between interior and exterior spaces.

134

135

Media Five Limited

345 QUEEN STREET, SUITE 900
HONOLULU, HAWAII 96813

THE **HYATT REGENCY** TUMON BAY, GUAM

At Media Five Limited design is a total concept. For this reason the total scope of design is offered, including architecture, interior design, planning, programming, and project management. For over 25 years, these multi-disciplinary capabilities have provided clients a significant advantage in project management, coordination and delivery. As a result, the firm is better equipped to meet a client's specific needs, for projects that range from multi-component luxury resorts, to private residences, to corporate offices. Every project makes an essential design statement that is appropriate, special, and above all, personal.

Media Five has evolved and grown to be a center for design in the Pacific. It has achieved this goal on the strength of its superior performance, the talent and teamwork of its people, and the trust it has garnered in the business of design.

The varied interiors of the Hyatt Regency Guam present strong architectural statements with a contemporay and exciting look.

137

Circular volumes and open truss forms reflect the angle of the mountainous terrain at the Gran Deco Hotel & Ski Resort. Natural materials, expansive windows, and open vistas help marry the interior to the exterior surroundings.

YOKOHAMA NEW GRAND INTER-CONTINENTAL HOTEL YOKOHAMA, JAPAN

ALL PHOTOS BY: MANNY HABRON, RON STARR; AND COURTESY OF THE HOTELS

Michael Graves Architect

341 NASSAU STREET
PRINCETON, NEW JERSEY 08540

FUKUOKA HYATT REGENCY HOTEL AND OFFICE BUILDING FUKUOKA, JAPAN

Michael Graves Architect has been cited by *The New York Times* as "truly the most original voice America has produced in some time." He has been at the forefront of architectural design since he began his practice in Princeton, New Jersey, in 1964.

Graves has received over 100 prestigious awards for his designs in architecture, interiors, products, and graphics. Among his high-profile projects in the United States alone are corporate headquarters for Humana, Crown American, the Disney Company, and Thomson Consumer Electronics. He has designed numerous office complexes, cultural facilities, and educational institutions. Graves' practice has become highly international, with completion of major projects in Japan, Europe, and the Middle East. Also well-known for his design of furniture, furnishings, and artifacts, Graves designs for Atelier International, Baldinger, Alessi, Steuben, Moller, and other manufacturers. Many of his products are marketed under the trademark Graves Design and are sold at retail establishments throughout the world.

He has extensive experience in designing hotels and related commercial and recreational facilities, such as retail stores, restaurants, conference centers, and golf clubs. The hotel types vary widely, and include small-scale country clubs, business hotels, convention centers, and resorts. Each project is given a distinctive architectural character that is appropriate to its particular context. For all of these projects, Graves has been responsible for master planning and site design, architectural and interior design, and the selection or custom design of furniture, furnishings, graphics, and artwork.

Sited on a narrow in-fill lot, this project is a mixed-use development in the Japanese city of Fukuoka and includes a 260-room hotel and conference center with restaurants and shops. The hotel is within a thirteen-story and two six-story wings that join together to form an entrance court.

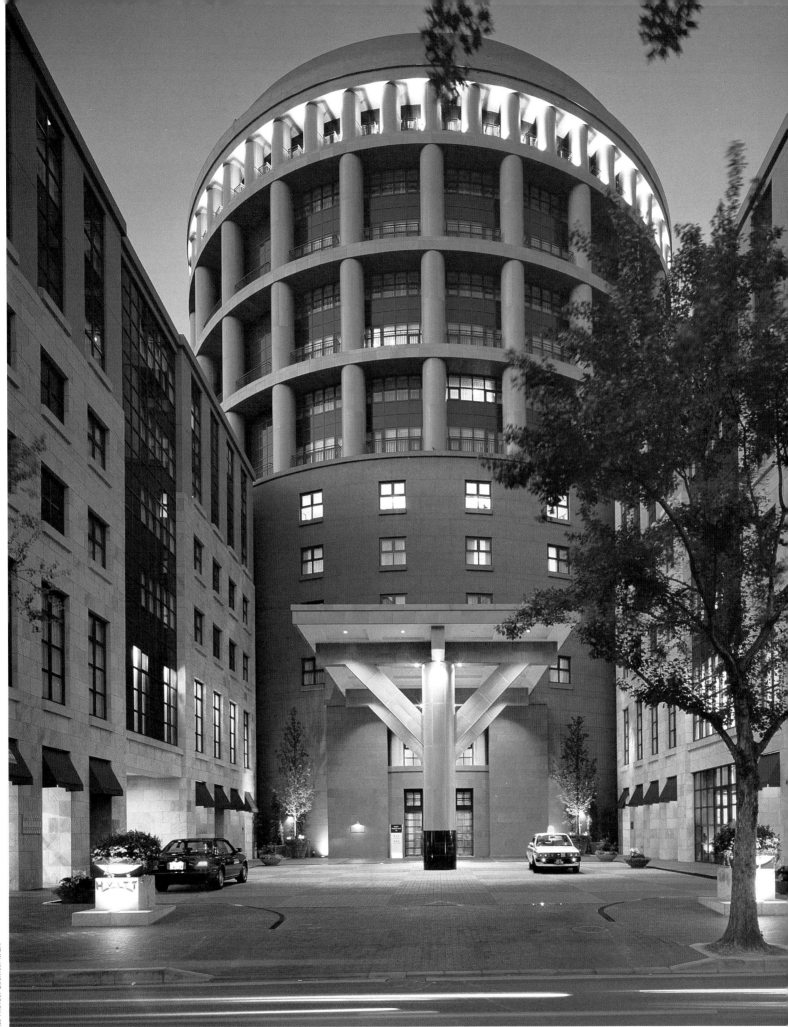

141

MICHAEL GRAVES ARCHITECT

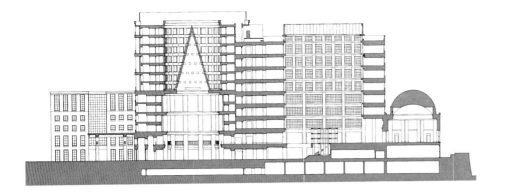

The hotel lobby, at the center of the rotunda, is lit from above by a dramatic pyramidal structure. The structure can also be viewed from the guest-room corridors in the rotunda.

The Fukuoka Hyatt Regency Hotel lobby
lounge, right, and drawing room,
above, show furniture and furnishings
custom designed by the architect.

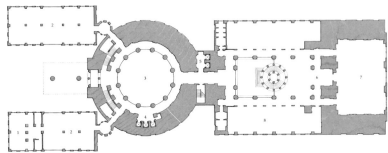

MICHAEL GRAVES ARCHITECT

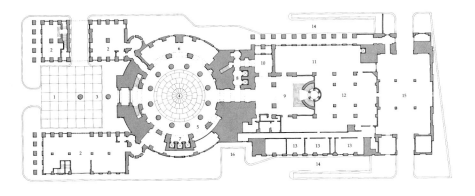

All Photos Courtesy MGA

145

MICHAEL GRAVES ARCHITECT

*The Miramar Hotel, in El Gouna, Egypt,
is a 284-room hotel located on the Red
Sea. The building's massing, character,
facades, and decorations are the architect's
interpretation of Egyptian traditions.*

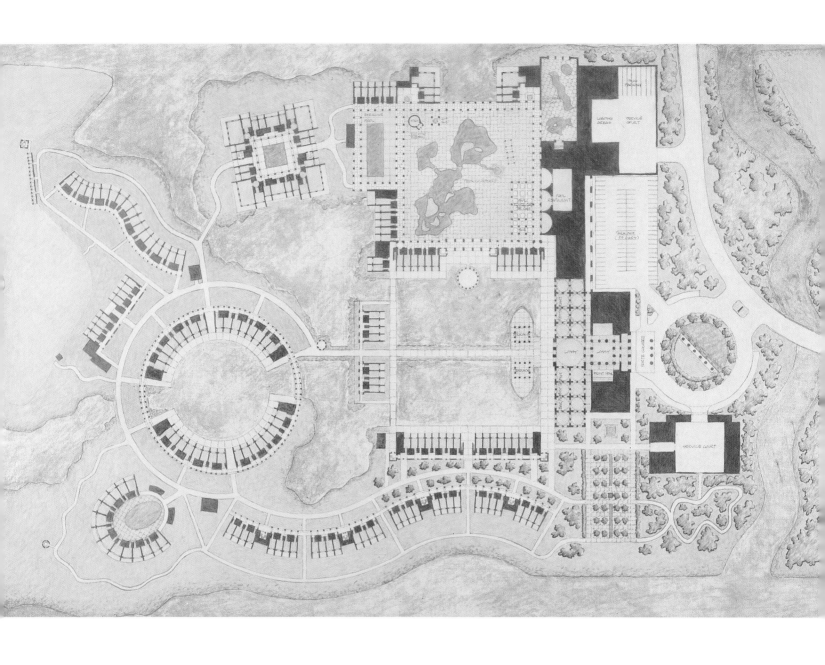

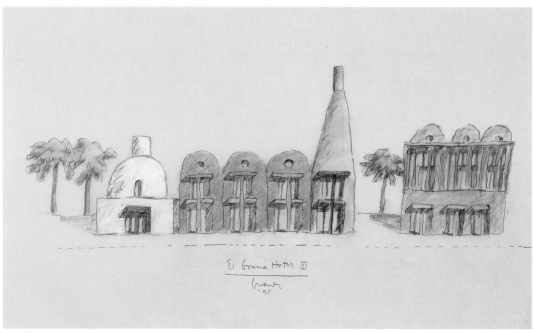

El Gouna Hotel III

The design for the hotel grounds takes advantage of the sea water as a landscape feature, with every guest room afforded a view of either the sea or the central swimming courtyard.

MICHAEL GRAVES ARCHITECT

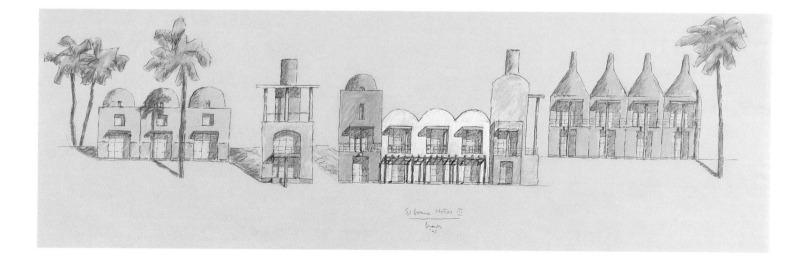

Parisi

2002 JIMMY DURANTE BOULEVARD, SUITE 308
DEL MAR, CALIFORNIA 92014

MT. WOODSON GOLF CLUB HOUSE   RAMONA, CALIFORNIA

Dedicated to creating environments in which elements with strong visual continuity are blended together, Parisi's hotel designs are intended to initiate journeys that capture guests' imaginations with subtle intrigue and unexpected detail. Parisi's designs are meant to be discovered. Their objective is to design functional space that evokes an emotional response, and sculpt spaces to deliver a sequential, progressive experience which draws travelers into the design's many textured and interpretive layers.

Historical and mythical influences meld with seemingly contradictory elements, of classic or contemporary styling underscored by rustic or primitive touches. Parisi visually expresses the belief that nature should be in harmony with their designs and integrated in their work. Using stone, glass, metals, woods, and textiles in unusual color palettes, they are able to create an elegant warmth and familiarity unique to each interior. Fully integrated design is this firm's calling card.

The design of the Mt. Woodson Hospitality Center was inspired by its historical site.

*A warm and sophisticated desert
ambiance greets guests at the Palobrea
Hospitality Residences at Big Horn
Golf Resort.*

PHOTOS BY: ED GOHLICH

153

The rotunda at the Villas of Renaissance are filled with natural light.

DESERT MOUNTAIN RESORT SANTA FE, NEW MEXICO

Rather than the typical cliché, a sophisticated Santa Fe–style prevails at the Sonoran Casitas at Desert Mountain Resort.

MIRADA HOSPITALITY CENTER RANCHO MIRAGE, CALIFORNIA

The Mirada at the Ritz Carlton, left, exhibits rich details, although in very different styles.

155

Pasanella + Klein Stolzman + Berg Architects

330 West 42nd Street
New York, New York 10036

Pasanella + Klein Stolzman + Berg Architects has a thirty-year history of award-winning architecture for a wide range of projects, including hotel, university-building, library, housing, office, residential, and medical interiors. They were given *Interiors Magazine*'s 1997 Best Hotel Award for the Mansfield Hotel. The firm is known for creating thoughtfully designed, meticulously crafted buildings, renovations, and interiors that critics have called sensitive, thoughtful, and perfect. Led by its three principals J. Arvid Klein, FAIA; Henry Stolzman, AIA; and Wayne Berg, FAIA; Pasanella + Klein Stolzman + Berg is a mid-size firm of 20 architects and designers. They are guided by the belief that good architecture must be satisfying, not only on its own aesthetic terms, but also as part of a larger context.

Additional recent distinctions include the 1996 National American Institute of Architects Honor Award for the Root House, in Ormond Beach, Florida and a 1995 *Progressive Architecture Magazine* Citation for the Education and Development Center at Clinch Valley College of the University of Virginia.

The welcoming details and sophisticated design of the reclaimed Mansfield Hotel are evident in the graciously reclaimed lobby and exterior entry, above and far right. Compare this to the previous condition, right.

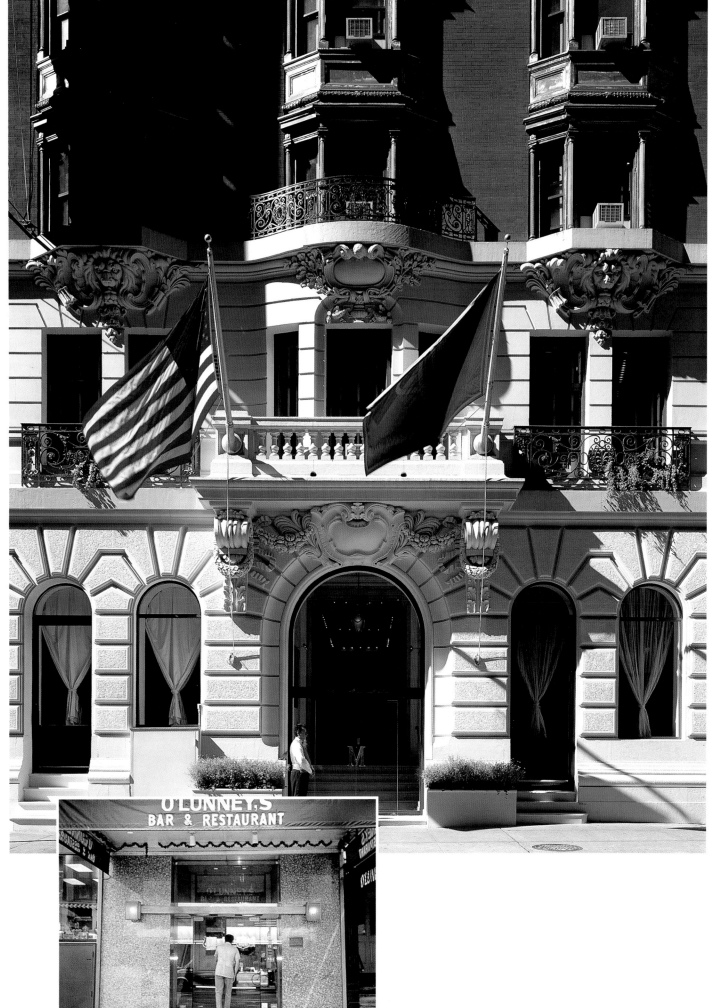

157

158

Beautiful details of the original building were recaptured throughout the hotel, as seen here in the reception area. The "before" view shows the same space after years of misguided "modernizations" left it in a bleak and sorry state. The tasteful comfort of the public spaces is seen above and right.

159

The penthouse suites' earlier loft and living
areas were renovated to become an upscale
two-level suite, above.

PASANELLA + KLEIN STOLZMAN + BERG ARCHITECTS

Ornate ceilings were preserved throughout the hotel.

PASANELLA + KLEIN STOLZMAN + BERG ARCHITECTS

In the transformation from a rundown crack house to a high-design but low-budget hotel, the designers used low-cost materials for custom-designed furnishings, repeating the use of tubular steel frames and cherry plywood throughout.

PASANELLA + KLEIN STOLZMAN + BERG ARCHITECTS

Pasanella + Klein Stolzman + Berg Architects

Mithun Partners

44 OLIVE WAY, SUITE 500
SEATTLE, WASHINGTON 98101

For close to 50 years, Mithun Partners has strongly influenced the built environment of the Northwest. With a rare commitment to architectural excellence, Mithun Partners has developed a staff that combines creativity, enthusiasm, and experience.

From an original staff of three in 1949, Mithun Partners has gradually expanded to its present level of 85, including 37 registered architects. This staffing level is large enough to respond quickly to projects of any size, yet small enough to provide personal service to clients. The firm's annual construction volume of $140 million includes architectural, interior design, and planning services.

Mithun Partners has been recognized by the American Institute of Architects, *Progressive Architecture* magazine, and *Architectural Record* magazine for design excellence in meeting programmatic and aesthetic criteria.

SALISH LODGE SPA ADDITION SNOQUALIMIE, WASHINGTON

This intimate mountain retreat rests at the crest of a 270-foot waterfall at the beginning of the Cascades. The shingle-style architectural character of the Spa addition is in keeping with the original architecture of the Salish Lodge designed by Mithun Partners nearly a decade ago. The scale and character of the spaces, a warm Northwest palette of natural materials, and a country inn appearance foster a peaceful retreat.

The combination of indigenous materials with Japanese references and forms captures the essence of a sanctuary.

Peter Gisolfi Associates

566 WARBURTON AVENUE
HASTINGS-ON-HUDSON, NEW YORK 10706

CASTLE AT TARRYTOWN TARRYTOWN, NEW YORK

Peter Gisolfi Associates has been providing service to the hospitality industry as well as other public and private clients since 1975. The combined talents of a 32-person office of architects, landscape architects, and interior architects provide completely integrated design services, from site selection through installation of furniture and accessories.

These professionals pride themselves on developing solutions that are compatible with both their natural and man-made surroundings. From examining historic precedents of a building type or environment, to analyzing local climates for energy-efficient design, to studying the ecosystem of a particular site, Peter Gisolfi Associates finds solutions for each project within the context of its unique environment.

The primary function of architecture is to make spaces. The firm's approach to design is based on the integration of buildings with site to create clearly defined and harmonious indoor and outdoor spaces. Among the firm's projects are hotels and restaurants, commercial buildings and office spaces, institutional and municipal buildings, housing complexes, houses, gardens, parks, recreational facilities, urban spaces, and master plans.

Originally built between 1900 and 1910, the fortress-like structure of the Castle at Tarrytown was inspired by the Norman fortifications of Wales, Scotland, and Ireland. The architects added new stonework to the exterior, and enclosed a porte-cochere to create a main entrance.

*Much of the interiors were recreated
by Gisolfi, including elaborate interior
finishes and details.*

PETER GISOLFI ASSOCIATES

Each of the guest suites were individually designed and furnished.

PETER GISOLFI ASSOCIATES

Once an outside porch, the Terrace Dining Room was enclosed.

PETER GISOLFI ASSOCIATES

Wimberly Allison Tong & Goo Architects and Planners

700 BISHOP STREET, SUITE 1800
HONOLULU, HAWAII 96813

Wimberly Allison Tong & Goo (WAT&G), with offices in Honolulu, Newport Beach, London, and Singapore, is recognized as the world's leading architecture firm specializing in hotel and resort planning and design. Since its founding in 1945, the firm has worked in 114 countries and territories on six continents, with projects throughout the Pacific Rim, the U.S. mainland, Mexico, South America, the Caribbean, Europe, Africa, and the Middle East.

WAT&G's expertise centers around the planning, design, and renovation of hospitality and leisure-oriented facilities, including urban and resort hotels, theme-entertainment centers, recreational facilities, golf and resort residential communities, casinos, spas, timeshare resorts, and convention facilities.

PHOTO BY: BERGER/CONSER

WAT&G's projects have been widely acclaimed: the firm has been the recipient of many prestigious design awards, and has been featured in over 175 publications worldwide. WAT&G's policy is to respect the environment and cultural heritage of each host community. This distinctive sense of place is integral to WAT&G projects throughout the world.

Australia's first health management residential resort was modeled on a village plan. A village square serves as entry lobby, above. Here guests can shop, eat, or relax.

175

Interior spaces were not only completely reconfigured, but also reoriented to showcase the Prince Felipe, Hyatt, La Manga Club's leisure facilities and amenities, right and below. The architects stripped the original 1970s Modernist hotel to its structure, than started anew to create a Spanish villa-like resort.

PRINCE FELIPE, HYATT LA MANGA CLUB, LA MANGA, SPAIN

WIMBERLY ALLISON TONG & GOO ARCHITECTS AND PLANNERS

Dining rooms and other public spaces are an upbeat mix of classic and contemporary design.

When WAT&G renovated the Orchid only six years after their original design was constructed, it was to satisfy the requirements of the hotel's new owners for a luxurious, but less formal and characteristically tropical, ambiance.

ALL PHOTOS BY: MILROY/MCALEER

After the government of the Bahamas sold off its hotels to private interests, the inventory was in less than stellar shape. At the Atlantis, Paradise Island Resort & Casino, the architects chose a renewal concept based on water. Buildings within the 14-acre water-scape were renovated within less than 10 months into a resort that reflects sea life and other marine aspects of the Caribbean.

179

A U-shaped plan and elevated central pool terrace keep guest views focused away from a nearby highway. Each guest room in the 12-story tower of the Waterfront Hilton Beach Resort is afforded a panoramic ocean view.

PHOTO BY ROBERT MILLER

The design of the Four Seasons Hotel
Mexico City takes a bow to both Spanish
Colonial and historic French architecture.
A colonnade-surrounded courtyard
bespeaks Mexico's heritage.

WIMBERLY ALLISON TONG & GOO ARCHITECTS AND PLANNERS

ALL PHOTOS BY BRUCE STANFORD

WIMBERLY ALLISON TONG & GOO ARCHITECTS AND PLANNERS

Environmental mitigation was the driving
force behind the plan for the Ritz-Carlton,
St. Thomas. The desire to preserve the
ecologically important site led to a design
that divides the resort into low, small-scale
components—six guest buildings and a
separate dining facility. Materials complement the Mediterranean-style architecture.

PMG Architects

156 5TH AVENUE
NEW YORK, NEW YORK 10010

DELANO HOTEL MIAMI BEACH, FLORIDA

PMG Architects was established in 1992 as a full-service architectural firm. Principal Peter Michael Gumpel has over 25 years experience in virtually every building type, from housing to hotels, including commercial, health care, academic, transportation, and civic facilities.

Focusing on the problem-solving aspect of architecture, PMG Architects examines each project as a unique set of issues to be analyzed, evaluated, and formulated into a solution that satisfies the functional, fiscal, and aesthetic goals of the client. The award-winning firm specializes in renovating, restoring, and rehabilitating hospitality buildings. Renovation of the Delano Hotel in Miami Beach was recently completed with designer Phillipe Starck, and PMG Architects is currently renovating the lobby of the Madison Towers Hotel.

ALL PHOTOS COURTESY OF DELANO HOTEL

The 208-room Art Deco Delano, set in the heart of Miami Beach, has undergone extensive renovation. Working with designer Phillipe Starck, the architects worked to undo the hotel's modernizations, capturing instead the casual glamour of Miami Beach.

185

Instead of the expected hotel lobby, Delano's front door opens onto a multi-faceted indoor/outdoor lobby comprised of eight distinct areas, with no formal definitions to separate them. Dramatic and quiet resting spots are included, right, along with places to eat, such as the Rose Bar, left, and the Breakfast Room, below.

PMG ARCHITECTS

188

Outdoor eating areas in the orchard continue the theme of the indoor/outdoor lobby.

Studio Sofield Inc.

380 LAFAYETTE STREET, PENTHOUSE NO. 2
NEW YORK, NEW YORK 10003

When designer William Sofield revived his downtown studio in 1996, he envisioned a workplace dedicated to the cultivation of close, creative relationships with a select group of clients and a resource of artisans. These priorities inspire the full range of design services that Studio Sofield provides. Sofield has developed expertise in all aspects of retail and hospitality design, as well as residential and garden design. An alliance of functional design and artistic vision characterizes all of Sofield's work, resulting in singular design concepts, thoughtful detail, and unsurpassed quality.

William Sofield entered the design field over a decade ago, establishing his own practice in 1989. Early on, Sofield was noted for his range of work and for his sensitivity to materials, finishes, and other integral elements. In 1992, Sofield co-founded Aero Studios, a design firm that offered its own line of custom furniture and accessories. In this context, Sofield upheld the Bauhaus philosophy of contemporary design that integrates the requirements of everyday life with craft tradition. In his new studio, Sofield continues to pay close attention to the needs and aesthetic preferences of his clients, in order to create spaces that best express function, context, and identity.

Inspired by the vast, columned interiors of SoHo's nineteenth century industrial buildings, the contemporary design of the SoHo Grand celebrates the period with colossal masonry columns, exposed beams, and a luminous cast iron and bottle glass staircase suspended from the lobby's two-story ceiling.

191

The historical, industrial theme is referred
to throughout. Even the contemporary
elegance of the guest rooms is punctuated
with Stickley-era type furniture and
furnishings.

ALL PHOTOS: COURTESY OF STUDIO SOFIELD

Tadao Ando Architect & Associates

5-23 TOYOSAKI 2-CHOME, KITA-KU
OSAKA, 531 JAPAN

NAOSHIMA CONTEMPORARY ART MUSEUM AND HOTEL BENESSE ISLAND, JAPAN

Tadao Ando is a Japanese architect with his own aesthetic, derived from earth-wrought materials and reflections of natural shapes. In turn, he uses these shapes to celebrate air, water, and light. An artist in the medium of concrete, his buildings are characterized by graceful simplicity, pared down to only the essentials. The peacefulness of the spaces he designs is in part derived from a link of nature into the central theme of his architecture. The landscape is as much a part of his designs as the structure. Yet while the landscape is likely to flow and curve, he relies often on sharp angles and rigid geometric building forms that cast shadows and reflect light.

PHOTO BY TOMIO OHASHI

A self-taught architect, Tadao Ando was the 1995 Pritzker Prize recipient. In addition, he has been honored with numerous international awards and exhibitions of his work. The majority of his buildings are located in Japan, but he has also completed a project in Germany— the widely acclaimed Vitra Conference Center.

Both the gallery areas and the hotel lodgings of the Benesse House, Naoshima Contemporary Art Museum were partly submerged into a hillside overlooking the sea. The entire concrete and marble compound flows seamlessly together.

PHOTO BY HIROSHI UEDA

TADAO ANDO ARCHITECT & ASSOCIATES

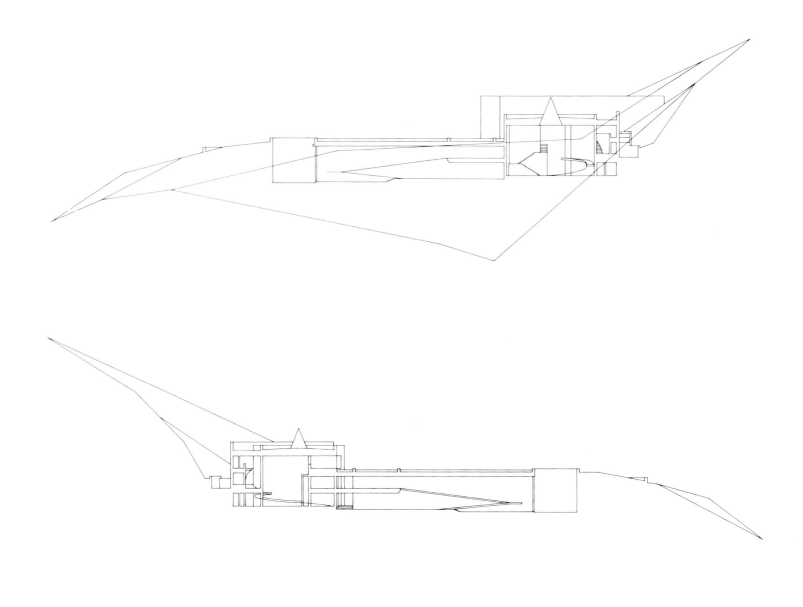

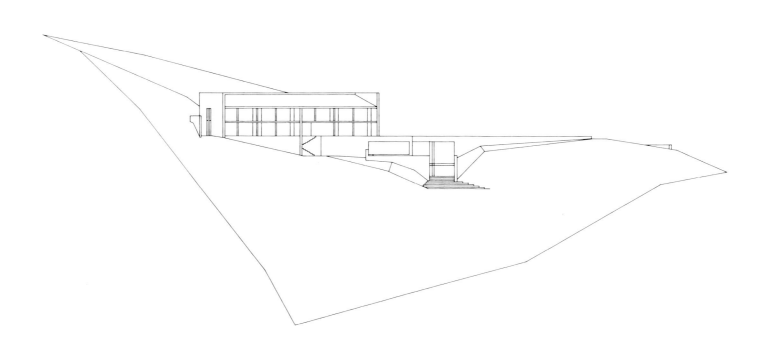

Tadao Ando Architect & Associates

Much of the museum, its annex, and the hotel lodgings were designed to overlook layers of grass and the Setonaikai Sea.

197

Located up a hill from the museum is a new hotel annex, an elliptical volume surrounding an internal pond cut into the ground, that provides 6 more rooms, in addition to the 10 in the main hotel.

199

From outdoors, walkways and patios
seem to hover above the ocean, while at
the same time they are securely embraced
by surrounding terraces of earth.

TADAO ANDO ARCHITECT & ASSOCIATES

Furniture in the museum and guest rooms was designed by Tadao Ando. Concrete, wood, and double-paned windows are themes repeated throughout.

Texeira, Inc.

717 NORTH LA CIENEGAL
LOS ANGELES, CALIFORNIA 90069

Texeira, Inc. brings international expertise, many years of experience and a fresh approach to every aspect of its work. Founded in 1983 by Glenn Texeira and consistently ranked in the "top ten" interior design firms, the firm is headquartered in Los Angeles and provides a full range of interior design services, from interior architecture to interior design, space planning, conceptual development and detailing of finishes, custom designed carpet and furnishings, purchasing, and installation.

Glenn Texeira and his associates work closely with each client to understand the special needs and marketing goals identified for each project. Texeira desires to be fully informed about the market niche, budget, and long-term business plan for the hotel before beginning the conceptual design process. The firm is skilled at bringing forth concepts that embody the client's vision as well as implementing the design process in-house. Although the firm's work is remarkably diverse, the hand-tailored quality, understated appropriateness, and infusion of regional characteristics are trademarks of every installation.

Evaluations of their work show that their designs are psychological successes as well as aesthetic successes.

Texeria, Inc. has many talented designers on staff who have created one-of-a-kind pieces for their interiors. From precisely detailed casegoods to the design of a signature chair for a hotel lobby, they have been inspired to create originals. Their designs transcend any particular style: they are simply graceful and comfortable in appearance and in performance.

Texeria, Inc. has developed contemporary and economical means of detailing age-old aesthetic emblems that emphasize mastery and proficiency in all design disciplines.

The Gettys Group, Inc.

801 EAST ILLINOIS STREET, SUITE 401
CHICAGO, ILLINOIS 60611

The Gettys Group is consistently recognized for award-winning hotel renovations. Winner of *Lodging Hospitality's Renovation Contest* in the mid-scale guest room category for 1994-1995, The Gettys Group concentrates on developing beautiful designs within limited budgets.

Budget-wise renovations have become part of the group's signature, which includes turn-key services. It is one of the only design, architecture, and purchasing firms that also offers management consulting. This unique management consulting creates value for clients. With its turn-key services, Gettys shepherds hotel companies through all phases of renovation, repositioning, or construction projects. It also offers operations and services assessments and audits.

In less than 10 years, The Gettys Group has achieved recognition as an industry leader. The company is ranked nationally among the top 10 lodging design firms, and as the sixth largest purchasing firm. Gettys was a 1995 Gold Key Awards finalist. Its clients include Hilton Hotels, Hyatt Hotels, Holiday Inns, Radisson Hotels, Sheraton Corporation, Days Inn, and Ritz Carlton.

ALL PHOTOS BY BRUCE VAN INWEGEN

*Renovation of The Radisson Plaza
in Indianapolis has created a more
unified and inviting internal image
for the hotel.*

207

THE GETTYS GROUP, INC.

Sophisticated interiors make this renovated suburban hotel distinctively different from its nearby competition.

209

At the Hyatt Regency Oak Brook, the proximity to Chicago drove the theme, as evidenced in the murals and artifacts.

*The nine-million dollar renovation of the
Radisson Hotel in Chicago was finished
within a year, with the hotel remaining
open throughout the process.*

Vivian/Nichols Associates, Inc.

2811 McKinney, Suite 302, LB 105
Dallas, Texas 75204

A succession of hotel and other leisure and gaming property designs throughout the United States has earned the interior architectural firm of Vivian/Nichols Associates, Inc., integral player status in these market segments. Vivian/Nichols Associates, Inc., was founded in 1985 by partners Dierdre Duchêne and Reggi Nichols-Hales. Over the past decade, the firm has created award-winning designs for prestigious hotels, lavish resorts, convention centers, historical restorations, and restaurants throughout North America. Vivian/Nichols Associates is recognized for their ability to consistently produce award-winning design, while executing each client's unique demands, respective of market and locale, within set financial guidelines. Their design philosophy and approach stems from a mixture of reality and fantasy giving each design its own imaginative identity. The spirit, dedication, and harmony of the firm's designers have earned Vivian/Nichols Associates, Inc. national recognition.

A reference to the atmosphere of a turn-of-the-century great lodge creates an understated mountain environment, replete with natural materials, warm colors, and commissioned nature and country artwork at the Houstonian Hotel and Conference Center.

All Photos by Michael French

Vivian/Nichols Associates, Inc.

PHOTO BY MICHAEL FRENCH

*Commanding three guest-room bays and
the penthouse, the Presidential Suite of the
Westchase Hilton lends itself to business
functions as well as an urban retreat.*

VIVIAN/NICHOLS ASSOCIATES, INC.

Reminiscent of the Texas hill country, the interior of the Hyatt Regency Austin is accented with sisal, hides, limestone, and iron. The Holiday Inn Select Dallas Central appears left.

HYATT REGENCY AUSTIN, TEXAS

215

Directory

Aiello Associates, Inc.
1525 Market Street
Suite A
Denver, Colorado 80202

Arquitectonica
550 Brickell Avenue
Suite 200
Miami, Florida 33131

Arrowstreet Inc.
212 Elm Street
Somerville, Massachusetts 02144

Barry Design Associates, Inc.
10780 Santa Monica Boulevard
Suite 300
Los Angeles, California 90025

Birch Coffey Design Associates
206 East 63rd Street
Suite 3
New York, New York 10021

Brennan Beer Gorman/Architects;
Brennan Beer Gorman Monk/Interiors
515 Madison Avenue
New York, New York 10022

Cesar Pelli & Associates Architects, Inc.
1056 Chapel Street
New Haven, Connecticut 06510

Cheryl Rowley Interior Design
9538 Brighton Way
Suite 316
Beverly Hills, California 90210

Cooper Carry, Inc.
3520 Piedmont Road NE
Suite 200
Atlanta, Georgia 30305-1595

Design Continuum, Inc.
5 Piedmont Center
Suite 300
Atlanta, Georgia 30305

Di Leonardo International, Inc.
2350 Post Road
Warwick, Rhode Island 02886

Einhorn Yaffee Prescott Architecture
and Engineering
The Argus Building
Broadway at Beaver Street
Albany, New York 12201

Hamilton Hochheiser Ross
6011 Staples Mill Road
Richmond, Virginia 23228

Hill/Glazier Architects
700 Welch Road
Palo Alto, California 94304

HLW International
115 5th Avenue
New York, New York 10003

Hughes Design Associates
1487 Chain Bridge Road
McLean, Virginia 22101

Knauer Inc.
741 St. Johns Avenue
Highland Park, Illinois 60035

Media Five Limited
345 Queen Street
Suite 900
Honolulu, Hawaii 96813

Michael Graves Architect
341 Nassau Street
Princeton, New Jersey 08540

Mithun Partners
414 Olive Way
Suite 500
Seattle, WA 98101

Murphy/Jahn
35 East Wacker Drive
3rd Floor
Chicago, IL 60601

Pamela Temples Interiors Inc.
7652 Ashley Park Court
Suite 306
Orlando, Florida 32835

Parisi
2002 Jimmy Durante Boulevard
Suite 308
Del Mar, California 92014

Pasanella + Klein Stolzman + Berg
Architects
330 West 42nd Street
New York, New York 10036

Peter Gisolfi Associates
566 Warburton Avenue
Hastings-on-Hudson, New York 10706

PMG Architects
156 5th Avenue
New York, New York 10010

Robert A.M. Stern Architects
460 West 34th Street
New York, New York 10010

Sue Firestone & Associates
4141 State Street, Suite B-13
Santa Barbara, California 93110

Studio Sofield Inc.
380 Lafayette Street
Penthouse No. 2
New York, New York 10003

Tadao Ando Architect & Associates
5-23 Toyosaki 2-chome, Kita-ku
Osaka, 531 Japan

Texeira, Inc.
717 North La Cienega
Los Angeles, California 90069

The Gettys Group, Inc.
801 East Illinois Street
Suite 401
Chicago, Illinois 60611

Vivian/Nichols Associates, Inc.
2811 McKinney
Suite 302, LB 105
Dallas, Texas 75204

Wilson & Associates
3811 Turtle Creek Boulevard
Dallas, Texas 75219

Wimberly Allison Tong & Goo
Architects and Planners
700 Bishop Street
Suite 1800
Honolulu, Hawaii 96813

Walt Disney Imagineering
1401 Flower Street
Glendale, CA 91221-5020